Grade 4

300 Brain-Stretching Challenges for Language Arts, Math, Geography and More...

Michelle Ball & Barbara Morris

These popular teacher resources and activity books are available from
ECS Learning Systems, Inc., for Grades K-6.

ECS1928	Get Writing!!™ Sentences	96pp.	Gr. K
ECS1936	Get Writing!!™ Sentences & Paragraphs	128pp.	Gr. 1
ECS1944	Get Writing!!™ Book 1: Sentences & Mechanical Control	128pp.	Gr. 2-3
ECS1952	Get Writing!!™ Book 2: Paragraphs & Forms of Writing	160pp.	Gr. 2-3
ECS1960	Get Writing!!™ Book 1: Main Ideas in Sentences	144pp.	Gr. 4-5
ECS1979	Get Writing!!™ Book 2: Main Ideas in Paragraphs	144pp.	Gr. 4-5
ECS1073	The Little Red Writing Book™	144pp.	Gr. 1-2
ECS1081	The Little Red Writing Book™	144pp.	Gr. 3-4
ECS109X	The Little Red Writing Book™	144pp.	Gr. 5-6
ECS1103	The Bright Blue Thinking Book™	144pp.	Gr. 1-2
ECS1111	The Bright Blue Thinking Book™	144pp.	Gr. 3-4
ECS1124	The Bright Blue Thinking Book™	144pp.	Gr. 5-6
ECS1790	Inkblots™	112pp.	Gr. K-3
ECS1804	Inkblots™	128pp.	Gr. 4-6
ECS9072	Writing Warm-Ups™	80pp.	Gr. K-6
ECS9455	Writing Warm-Ups™	80pp.	Gr. K-6
ECS9692	Springboards for Reading	96pp.	Gr. 3-6
ECS9471	Quick Thinking	80pp.	Gr. K-6
ECS1030	Math Whiz Kids™ at the Amusement Park	80pp.	Gr. 3-5
ECS1057	Math Whiz Kids™ at Home	80pp.	Gr. 3-5
ECS1065	Math Whiz Kids™ at the Mall	80pp.	Gr. 3-5
ECS1049	Math Whiz Kids™ at the Zoo	80pp.	Gr. 3-5
NU783XRH	Graphic Organizer Collection	144pp.	Gr. 3-12

To order, or for a complete catalog, write:

ECS Learning Systems, Inc.
P.O. Box 440
Bulverde, Texas 78163-0440

Web site: www.educyberstor.com
or contact your local school supply store.

Editor: Shirley J. Durst
Cover Design and Page Layout: Anh N. Le

ISBN 1-57022-227-4

Copyright infringement is a violation of Federal Law.

© 2000, 2004 by ECS Learning Systems, Inc., Bulverde, Texas. All rights reserved. No part of this publication may be reproduced, translated, stored in a retrieval system, or transmitted in any way or by any means (electronic, mechanical, photocopying, recording, or otherwise) without prior written permission from ECS Learning Systems, Inc.

Photocopying of student worksheets by a classroom teacher at a non-profit school who has purchased this publication for his/her own class is permissible. Reproduction of any part of this publication for an entire school or for a school system, by for-profit institutions and tutoring centers, or for commercial sale is strictly prohibited.

Printed in the United States of America.

Table of Contents

About this Book

Wake Up, Brain!! Activities 6

Answer Key 106

About the Authors 112

About this Book

My inspiration for *Wake Up, Brain!!* came when I was challenged to keep track of the grammar, spelling, language, geography, and math concepts taught in my multi-age classroom. As an organizational tool, I created mini lesson plans for tracking curriculum elements for each grade or skill level. The plan included activities in five different curricular areas, plus one riddle.

My co-author, Barbara Morris, created a student- and teacher-friendly format on her computer. As time passed, we wrote more and more activities for grades 1, 2, and 3, and eventually created *Wake Up, Brain!!* for grades 4, 5, and 6, as well.

I use *Wake Up, Brain!!* as my daily mini lesson plan and expand the ideas in detail on the chalkboard or in class discussion. What a time-saver! No researching ideas or deciding what lessons to use. Students can finish all 5 activities and try to solve the riddle in as little as 5 to ten minutes.

Kids love *Wake Up, Brain!!*, too. I am constantly amazed and delighted at how practice with these mini-lessons enhances student learning in the individual subject areas. It only took a week or two for my students to get accustomed to reviewing the five subject areas at once. Now it's one of their favorite ways to learn!

Michelle Ball

Each book in the Wake Up, Brain!! series covers the necessary elements for teaching grammar, language, spelling, geography, and math for a specific grade level. Whether you are a teacher in a traditional or multi-age classroom, a homeschooler, or a parent wanting to become more involved in your child's school work, *Wake Up, Brain!!* is for you.

Use *Wake Up, Brain!!* for—

- ✦ graded daily mini-lessons
- ✦ teacher-led or independent practice
- ✦ group practice
- ✦ assessment of student skills, including special needs
- ✦ reinforcement of essential concepts
- ✦ homework, extra credit, or quizzes
- ✦ acquainting parents with the basic curriculum

Wake Up, Brain!!

Name: _____

Grammar

1. jamie eated all the ben and jerrys ice cream

   _____

   _____

2. do you have time to take a shower before we go

   _____

   _____

Spelling

Which of these words is spelled correctly?

3. gim   gym   jym   _____

4. favrite   favorit   favorite   _____

5. thought   thot   thoght   _____

Language

Finish the following analogies.

6. **Up** is to **down** as **in** is to _____

7. **Over** is to **under** as **top** is to _____

8. **Month** is to **year** as **week** is to _____

Wake Up, Brain!!

Name: _____

Geography

1. If you are facing south, which direction is to your left?
   _____

2. Which country has more land, the U.S. or Mexico?
   _____

Math

KEVIN SAVED $25.00

3. Does he have enough money to buy a skateboard for $20.00, a toy car for $3.50, and a hamburger for $3.00?

   ❏ No   ❏ Yes   How much change? _____

4. Does he have enough money to buy a $7.00 book and a $16.00 CD?

   ❏ No   ❏ Yes   How much change? _____

5. What has a head like a cat, eyes like a cat, a tail like a cat, but isn't a cat?
   _____

A kitten.

Wake Up, Brain!!

Name: _____

Grammar

1. lets have soup sandwiches and chips for saturdays lunch

   _____

   _____

2. i cant seem to keep my room clean can you

   _____

   _____

Spelling

Write a word that describes each picture.

3. _____ 4. _____ 5. _____

Language

6. List three items under each category.

GAMES	PETS	RELATIVES

Wake Up, Brain!!

Name: _____

Geography

1. Which of these is not a state?

   Georgia   Tennessee   Indianapolis   Utah

2. What states border California to the east?
   _____

Math

$3 $8 $15

3. How much is the book and skateboard? _____

4. What's your change from $20 if you buy the basketball? _____

5. Why don't bananas ever get lonely?
   _____
   _____

Because they go around in bunches.

Wake Up, Brain!!

Name: _____

Grammar

1. her and her family invited me to go to church with them
   _____
   _____

2. we saw the president of the united states at the parade
   _____
   _____

Spelling

Write a word that describes each picture.

3. _____ 4. _____ 5. _____

Language

Millions of years ago, the Iguanodon roamed the earth. The Iguanodon was a plant eater. It looked like a giant lizard and had tough skin like leather.

6. The main idea is: _____

7. Iguanodons ate: _____

8. The skin was: _____

Wake Up, Brain!!

Name: _____

Geography

1. What symbol usually shows a state's capital city?
   _____

2. How many continents are there in the world?

   16   50   7   1

Math

3. How much money is this? _____

4. One bike costs $89.50. How much are two bikes?
   _____

5. What is another name for a phone booth?
   _____
   _____

A chatterbox.

Wake Up, Brain!!

Name: _____

Grammar

1. well go to california this summer we might go to disneyland to

   _____

   _____

2. my chores is to take out the trash make my bed mow the lawn and walk the dog

   _____

   _____

Spelling

3. Underline the misspelled words then spell them correctly in the boxes below.
   Evrything we tried doesnt work. We don't know who can help us exsept my brother.

Language

Kareem Abdul-Jabbar grew up in New York City. He grew to be more than 7 feet tall! He played basketball in high school and in college, too. Now his job is playing professional basketball.

4. The main idea is: _____

5. When did Kareem play basketball? _____

Wake Up, Brain!!

Name: _____

Geography

1. What color do you see most on a map of the world?
   _____
   _____

2. What does that color represent?
   _____
   _____

Math

3. Circle the shapes you need to draw an ice cream cone.

4. Why shouldn't you believe a person in bed?
   _____
   _____

Because he/she is lying.

Wake Up, Brain!!

Name: _____

Grammar

1. why dont we go see dr doolittle together wed have a great time

   _____ _____

   _____

2. please put them pencils in the box them books on the shelfs and them papers in the trash

   _____

   _____

Spelling

Unscramble these words.

3. trigh _____

4. nufod _____

Language

5. List three items under each category.

BOARD GAMES	CITIES	STATES

Wake Up, Brain!!

Name: _____

Geography

1. Do temperatures get warmer or cooler as you get closer to the equator?
   _____

2. A _____ is a line on a map that marks the spot where one place starts and another ends.

Math

Basketball $12   Skateboard $25   T-shirt $32

3. What is the difference between the cost of the t-shirt and the skateboard?
   _____

4. What's your change from $20 if you buy the basketball?
   _____

5. What kind of apple isn't an apple?
   _____
   _____

A pineapple.

Wake Up, Brain!!

Name: _____

Grammar

1. julie and me was going to the mall to like shop for school clothes

   _____

   _____

2. we drunk to much pop and gots a bellyache

   _____

   _____

Spelling

Choose the correct spelling of these words.

3. troubel   trubble   trouble   _____

4. doesn't   dosn't   does'nt   _____

5. exsited   excited   excitet   _____

Language

6. Circle the action verbs.

   Jamie and Sam are in line to go on the roller coaster. They have never been on such a big ride before. Jamie is biting her lip and Sam is feeling warm. "Are you scared?" says Jamie. "Not at all! Are you?" lied Sam.

Wake Up, Brain!!

Name: _____

Geography

1. Continents are the largest bodies of _____?_____ on Earth.

   _____

2. The imaginary line that circles the middle of Earth is:

   _____

Math

3. Seth has 94 baseball cards. He traded 5 for one special card. How many does he have now?

4. 4 cups = _____ pints

5. 16 quarts = _____ gallons

6. What is the left side of an apple?

   _____
   _____

The part you don't eat.

Wake Up, Brain!!

Name: _____

Grammar

1. my uncle has an orchard with peach trees apple trees and lemon trees

   _____
   _____

2. have you saw the movie called a bugs life

   _____
   _____

Spelling

3. Circle words that would be between **floor** and **funny** in the dictionary.

flower	fan
flame	frame
fun	female
fancy	flown

Language

4. Circle the verbs in this recipe.

   Make a package of vanilla pudding.

   Slice half of a banana.

   Stir the banana slices into the pudding.

   Sprinkle crumbled graham crackers on top.

Wake Up, Brain!!

Name: _____

Geography

1. Name the seven continents of the world.

   _____ _____

   _____ _____

   _____ _____

   _____

Math

2. It's now 1:30. Jordan will leave to go to the library in 45 minutes. Circle the clock that shows what time it will be when Jordan leaves.

3. How do you stop a skunk from smelling?

   _____

   _____

Hold its nose.

Wake Up, Brain!!

Name: _____

Grammar

1. we runned around the hole playground for times

   _____

   _____

2. keith and erin doesnt like pickles jim only likes them on hamburgers i love them on

   everything _____

   _____

Spelling

Which of these words are spelled correctly?

3. The pirates found a _____ treasure.

       goldin   gulden   goalden   golden

4. The old car engine made a loud _____.

       raquet   raket   rackit   racket

Language

Which word has the **same** or **almost the same** meaning as the bolded word?

5. **mail**   ❏ letter   ❏ man   ❏ movie

6. **peace**   ❏ calm   ❏ officer   ❏ part

7. **fierce**   ❏ roar   ❏ sound   ❏ scary

Wake Up, Brain!!

Name: _____

Geography

1. Is the North Pole on a continent?   yes   no

2. Which state has the longest border on the Pacific Ocean?
   _____

Math

3. Draw a line from the figure to its matching word.

   Cylinder   Circle   Sphere   Cone   Triangle   Cube   Square

4. What kind of water can't freeze?
   _____
   _____

Hot water.

Wake Up, Brain!!

Name: _____

Grammar

1. did you no he hided the car behind the tree i cant believe we didnt find it

   _____

   _____

2. she drunk all her milk at dinner and then asked for more later

   _____

   _____

Spelling

Which word is spelled correctly?

3. ❏ outcide ❏ outside ❏ oteside

4. ❏ espesially ❏ especialy ❏ especially

5. ❏ somtime ❏ sumtime ❏ sometime

Language

Draw lines to each word's synonym.

6. forest   tired

7. sleepy   jogged

8. jacket   woods

9. ran   coat

Wake Up, Brain!!

Name: _____

Geography

1. Name the earth's four oceans.

   _____   _____

   _____   _____

2. How many states in the U.S. touch one another?

   ☐ 50   ☐ 49   ☐ 48   ☐ 47

Math

3. 184
   −140
   ____

4. 388
   −119
   ____

5. 1,892
   −1,782
   _____

6. 41 + 44 + 18 + 82 − 61 = _____

7. Why should you never wear polka dots when you play hide and seek?

   _____

   _____

You'll be spotted.

Wake Up, Brain!!

Name: _____

Grammar

1. my cats they love to wrestle and hiss at each other it looks like fighting but its not

   _____

   _____

2. is you grandparents arriving on the 600 am flight

   _____

   _____

Spelling

Write a word that describes each picture.

3. _____ 4. _____ 5. _____

Language

Draw a line from the adjective to the noun it describes, like this:

A platypus has a broad tail like a beaver.

6. These unusual mammals lay eggs.

7. Their webbed feet help them swim.

Wake Up, Brain!!

Name: _____

Geography

1. A body of land surrounded by water is:

   _____

2. What two oceans border Europe?

   ☐ Atlantic   ☐ Pacific   ☐ Arctic   ☐ Indian

Math

The bakery had 1426 sugar cookies and 1622 chocolate chip cookies.

3. What is the difference in the number of chocolate chip cookies and sugar cookies?

   _____

4. How many cookies all together? _____

5. How can you make seven even?

   _____

Take away the S.

Wake Up, Brain!!

Name: _____

Grammar

1. at summer camp we all rided horses except frank hed been bucked off before and was afraid _____
   _____

2. those cars are going to crash yelled james watch out
   _____
   _____

Spelling

Write the contraction for these words.

3. cannot _____
4. does not _____
5. would not _____

Language

Name the categories by reading the words.

6.	7.	8.
teachers	corn	Collie
playground	beans	Dalmatian
books	peas	Terrier

Wake Up, Brain!!

Name: _____

Geography

1. On what continent is the South Pole located?
   _____

2. Which is usually larger, a sea or an ocean?
   _____

Math

Draw the clock hands to show the correct time.

   3. 4:17   4. 12:09

5. What birds are always unhappy?
   _____

Bluebirds.

Wake Up, Brain!!

Name: _____

Grammar

1. grace and me went to see joels new bike its a cool racing bike

   _____

   _____

2. teresa brang her lunch today said kim did you

   _____

   _____

Spelling

Which spelling is correct?

3. ❏ abowt   ❏ about   ❏ aboat

4. ❏ before   ❏ befor   ❏ befour

5. ❏ myselv   ❏ my self   ❏ myself

Language

Write two or more complete sentences using the two words given. Make each sentence at least six words long.

6. other, sports _____

   _____

   _____

Wake Up, Brain!!

Name: _____

Geography

1. Which of the following is NOT an ocean?

   ❏ Arctic   ❏ Bering   ❏ Indian   ❏ Pacific

2. What country is the closest southern neighbor for most of the U.S.?
   _____

Math

3. Today it is 90 degrees outside. Yesterday it was 85 degrees. Which day was warmer?

   ❏ today   ❏ yesterday   ❏ tomorrow

4. Connect the shapes that are congruent.

   ● □ ◆ ☆ ✧ ▲ ♥
   ■ ★ ♣ ○ ◇ ◆ ▼

5. What goes around in circles and makes kids happy?
   _____
   _____

A merry-go-round.

Wake Up, Brain!!

Name: _____

Grammar

1. he has drank all the milk and he has ate all the cookies he must have been very hungry

   _____

   _____

2. he drawed that picture all by hisself without ever looking up

   _____

   _____

Spelling

Write the contractions for these words.

3. did not _____

4. let us _____

5. they are _____

Language

Unscramble the sequence from greatest to least.

6. forty, twenty, sixty _____

7. most, least, same _____

8. whole, half, quarter _____

Wake Up, Brain!!

Name: _____

Geography

1. Are the Rocky Mountains east or west of the Mississippi River?
   _____

2. Three oceans border the U.S. What are they?

   _____   _____

   _____

Math

Monkey #1 collects 98 coconuts. Monkey #2 collects 53 and monkey #3 collects 79.

3. Monkey #1 got _____ more coconuts than monkey #2?

4. All together, the monkeys got _____ coconuts.

5. Why are most cows noisy?
   _____
   _____

Because they have horns.

Wake Up, Brain!!

Name: _____

Grammar

1. david gots a ferret and michael gots a guinea pig

   _____

   _____

2. rebecca has went to oregon for the summer shell be back in september

   _____

   _____

Spelling

Unscramble these school words and put them in alphabetical order.

3. tewri _____   _____

4. raethec _____   _____

5. drilhcen _____   _____

Language

Finish these sequences.

6. inch, foot, _____

7. July, August, _____

8. fourth, fifth, _____

Wake Up, Brain!!

Name: _____

Geography

1. The largest ocean in the world?
   _____

2. Which two continents make up a single large mass of land?

   ☐ Asia   ☐ Africa   ☐ Europe   ☐ Australia

Math

Write the name of each shape.

3. _____

4. _____

5. _____

6. What can you hold without touching it?
   _____
   _____

A conversation.

Wake Up, Brain!!

Name: _____

Grammar

1. she done her chores every day and new her mom would be happy

   _____

   _____

2. where did you go this weekend asked ben we went camping replied eddie

   _____

   _____

Spelling

Write the correct word in each sentence.

3. your or you're
   What is _____ name? _____ nice.

4. there or their
   Let's go over _____ to _____ place.

Language

Circle the word that acts as a noun in one sentence and as a verb in the other sentence.

5. We need to make a plan. We will plan our trip.

6. Make two sentences of your own using a word that works as a noun and a verb.

   _____

   _____

Wake Up, Brain!!

Name: _____

Geography

1. Which of the following is NOT a city?
   ☐ San Diego   ☐ Washington, D.C.   ☐ Kansas

2. What state's Pacific Ocean border is longer
   ☐ Washington   ☐ Oregon

3. What is the capital city of Kentucky?
   _____

Math

Write + or – in the boxes below.

4. 77 ☐ 12 = 65   5. 491 ☐ 302 = 793

6. 144 ☐ 4 = 140   7. 12 ☐ 37 = 49

8. What kind of animal tells little white lies?
   _____
   _____

An amphibian.

Wake Up, Brain!!

Name: _____

Grammar

1. linda doesnt gots a pencil box is it okay if she uses a pouch

   _____
   _____

2. he done his homework real good

   _____
   _____

Spelling

Change these words to include an ending of "**ing**."

3. run _____
4. come _____
5. add _____

Language

Join these sentences using **when** or **because**.

6. The dog got out. The boy opened the gate.

   _____

7. I divided my **apple** in half. I saw Tim wanted some.

   _____

Wake Up, Brain!!

Name: _____

Geography

1. Which state is bordered by two oceans?

    ❏ Maine ❏ Alaska ❏ Florida

2. What state is north of Pennsylvania?

    ❏ New Jersey ❏ Ohio ❏ New York

Math

3. How many numbers in the box are greater than 440?

   | 301 | 466 | 555 | 219 | 439 | 501 |

    ❏ 2 ❏ 3 ❏ 4 ❏ 5 ❏ 6

4. Aaron was the eleventh boy to go outside. How many boys went outside before him?

    ❏ 9 ❏ 10 ❏ 11 ❏ 12

5. What is a bee with a low buzz?

   _____
   _____

A mumble bee.

Wake Up, Brain!!

Name: _____

Grammar

1. patrick hasta practice his piano lessons every night for thirty minutes

   _____

   _____

2. donald went all by hisself to the mall and he got like lost

   _____

   _____

Spelling

Change these words to include an ending of "**ed**."

3. share _____

4. chop _____

5. spy _____

Language

Find two words that could be made into a contraction. Write the contraction after the sentence.

6. We were not sure it was right. _____

7. I cannot do it alone. _____

8. Mom said, "Do not go in." _____

Wake Up, Brain!!

Name: _____

Geography

1. Which state does NOT border Mexico?

   ❏ Texas ❏ Nevada ❏ Arizona

2. What state is north of South Dakota?

   ❏ North Dakota ❏ Utah ❏ Colorado

Math

3. How many numbers in the box are less than 4,400?

   | 3,010 | 4,660 | 5,550 | 2,190 | 4,390 | 5,010 |

   ❏ 2 ❏ 3 ❏ 4 ❏ 5 ❏ 6

4. The store had 90 bikes. Forty-eight were sold. What was left?

   ❏ 98 ❏ 42 ❏ 138 ❏ 19

5. What is a forum?

   _____
   _____

Two-um plus two-um.

Wake Up, Brain!!

Name: _____

Grammar

1. can we go to tony's house in tallahassee on the fourth of july

   _____

   _____

2. mary gots to assignments ready to turn in

   _____

   _____

Spelling

Write the correct form of the word in parentheses.

3. He didn't (no, know) what to do. _____

4. Will you (buy, by) me a bike? _____

5. Jack (threw, through) the ball. _____

Language

Name the categories.

6.	7.	8.
rose	cherries	12:30 a.m.
daffodil	grapes	9 o'clock
tulip	peaches	half past three

Wake Up, Brain!!

Name: _____

Geography

1. What is the capital of Illinois?

   ❏ Chicago   ❏ Springfield   ❏ Springtown

2. Does the Bering Sea touch the U.S.?   ❏ Yes   ❏ No

   Where? _____

Math

3. Circle what you would use to measure how much a tomato weighs.

4. Draw a square around what you would use to measure the size of your paper.

5. What happened to the wolf who fell into the washing machine?

   _____
   _____

He turned into a wash and werewolf.

Wake Up, Brain!!

Name: _____

Grammar

1. can you bring your book a cd and some pop to the party

   _____

   _____

2. my cat tigger is like a wild cat when he eats catnip

   _____

   _____

Spelling

Underline the misspelled words. Spell them correctly below.

I'm not shure what to get my freind for his birthday. Do you know if he wuold want a book?

3.	4.	5.

Language

Underline the words used incorrectly. Write the correct words in the boxes below.

I'm not sure what to get my friend for its birthday. Do you thought he would wants a book?

6.	7.	8.

Wake Up, Brain!!

Name: _____

Geography

1. Place the geographic directions on this compass.

Math

2. Make a red mark on this ruler at the 5 ½ mark.

3. Make a blue mark on this ruler at the 2 ¾ mark.

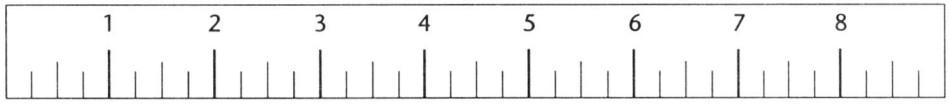

4. What is a sleeping bull?
   _____
   _____

A bull dozer.

Wake Up, Brain!!

Name: _____

Grammar

1. she dont want none on account of shes finished

   _____

   _____

2. did you get home late last night ask mom ben said just by 15 minutes mom

   _____

   _____

Spelling

Solve the riddle and spell the word.

3. Starts with R, ends with N,
   Falls down from a cloudy sky.

4. Has two Os in the center.
   It's what you should be.

Language

Put adjectives in the blanks to help the sentences.

5. Pete dropped his _____ coat.

6. Rebecca put _____ books away.

7. Four boys played with _____ cars.

Wake Up, Brain!!

Name: _____

Geography

1. Where is a home game played by the Miami Dolphins?

    ☐ Colorado   ☐ Florida   ☐ Oregon

2. In what state will you find San Francisco?

    ☐ Colorado   ☐ California   ☐ Connecticut

Math

The pet store has 122 betas, 114 guppies, and 136 goldfish.

3. How many fish are in the store altogether? _____

4. How many guppies and goldfish altogether? _____

5. What is the difference between the number of betas and the number of guppies?

    _____

6. How many peas are there in a pint?

    _____
    _____

There is only one P in pint.

Wake Up, Brain!!

Name: _____

Grammar

1. i used all my paper can i have more

   _____
   _____

2. ill pay you 25 cents a paper but i only gots 5 dollars

   _____
   _____

Spelling

Choose which word is spelled correctly.

3. ☐ somtime   ☐ sometime   ☐ sumtime

4. ☐ thought   ☐ thoght   ☐ thuoght

5. ☐ waether   ☐ weathor   ☐ weather

Language

Choose the best meaning of the bolded prefix.

6. **dis**honest   ☐ before   ☐ not   ☐ with

7. hope**less**   ☐ without   ☐ more   ☐ having

8. **dis**obey   ☐ very   ☐ opposite of   ☐ full of

Wake Up, Brain!!

Name: _____

Geography

1. Most of Yellowstone National Park is located in:

    ❏ Montana ❏ Wyoming ❏ Idaho

2. Your friend lives in the capital city of Augusta, what state does he or she live in?

    ❏ Missouri ❏ West Virginia ❏ Maine

Math

3. Circle the shapes that show lines of symmetry.

4. When can you jump while you're sitting down?

    _____
    _____

When you're playing checkers.

Wake Up, Brain!!

Name: _____

Grammar

1. we writted a note asking brandon who he liked the most

   _____

   _____

2. karen had like her feelings hurt because john was like go away

   _____

   _____

Spelling

Solve the riddles and spell the words.

3. Three letters for what you do at lunch;
   it rhymes with what's inside your shoes.

4. A word for "little" with two Ls at the end.

Language

Underline the simple subject of each sentence.

5. The birds ate the food from the birdhouse.

6. He caught a huge fish!

7. Rabbits ate all the carrots from the garden.

Wake Up, Brain!!

Name: _____

Geography

1. In what part of the U.S. is Colorado located?

   ❏ east   ❏ west   ❏ central

2. What is the capital of Tennessee?

   ❏ Nashville   ❏ New Orleans   ❏ Kansas City

Math

How many angles and how many sides are there to these shapes?

3. ▼ _____ angles _____ sides

4. ◆ _____ angles _____ sides

5. ⬣ _____ angles _____ sides

6. What do you use to comb a bee's hair?
   _____
   _____

A honeycomb.

Wake Up, Brain!!

Name: _____

Grammar

1. we seen the new baby panda at the zoo in june

   _____

   _____

2. weve had fun but now we has to go

   _____

   _____

Spelling

Underline the misspelled words and spell them correctly.

3. My sisster went to the movie. _____

4. Can you play owtside? _____

5. She was espeshelly nice. _____

Language

Underline the simple predicate of each sentence.

6. The car suddenly pulled into the driveway.

7. The bus stopped at the curb.

8. Roger gave the teacher the correct answer.

Wake Up, Brain!!

Name: _____

Geography

1. In what state would you be for a home game of the San Diego Padres?

   ☐ California   ☐ Oregon   ☐ Minnesota

2. What two states border Virginia to the south?

   ☐ Tennessee   ☐ North Carolina   ☐ Mississippi

Math

3. Circle the shapes that are divided into equal fourths.

4. Why couldn't the girl eat alphabet soup?
   _____
   _____

Because she was allergic to B's (bees).

Wake Up, Brain!!

Name: _____

Grammar

1. its way to early to wake up so i stayed in bed another our

   _____

   _____

2. did you laugh at bills joke i didnt think it was funny

   _____

   _____

Spelling

Write an antonym for these words.

3. gigantic _____

4. least _____

5. lost _____

Language

6. Write two sentences about this picture. Underline your nouns.

   _____

   _____

   _____

   _____

Wake Up, Brain!!

Name: _____

Geography

1. Which country has more land?

    ❏ Canada   ❏ United States   ❏ Russia

2. In what part of the country is West Virginia located?

    ❏ east   ❏ west   ❏ central

Math

Measure each line in centimeters. Write the length on the line.

3. _____

4. _____

5. _____

6. What planet is like a circus?
   _____
   _____

Saturn. It has 3 rings.

Wake Up, Brain!!

Name: _____

Grammar

1. wood you rather use the computer or a calculator

   _____

   _____

2. where has toby hid his bone he keeps digging more wholes

   _____

   _____

Spelling

Complete these sentences with words that rhyme with KITE.

3. I slept at grandma's house last _____ .

4. We should _____ her a thank you note.

5. He said, "Turn left!" I said, "Turn _____ !"

Language

6. Circle each word in the word box.

spider	a	c	t	a	r	c	j	w	c	s
star	k	h	m	b	p	m	l	s	d	t
noise	w	i	r	n	o	i	s	e	t	a
chin	c	n	i	r	s	p	i	d	e	r

Wake Up, Brain!!

Name: _____

Geography

1. What state is shaded?

   _____

Math

2. [array of stars] + [array of stars] + [array of stars] = _____

3. [array of stars] + [array of stars] + [array of stars] = _____

4. How do you make a peanut laugh?

   _____

   _____

You crack it up.

Wake Up, Brain!!

Name: _____

Grammar

1. dont you wish them kittens belonged to you and i
   _____
   _____

2. stephanie was like, "were gonna go to the mall
   _____
   _____

Spelling

Spell the past tense of each of these words.

3. want _____

4. tell _____

5. excite _____

Language

Circle the words that have the sound of the letter in the box.

6. | ă | bag   bake   brain   match

7. | ĕ | week   bread   wet   red

8. | ō | phone   chop   grow   dog

Wake Up, Brain!!

Name: _____

Geography

Name the major river that flows all the way through each state.

1. Idaho _____

2. Mississippi _____

3. Alaska _____

Math

4. Circle the numbers with an 8 in the tens place.

   8,989   4,828   5,181   3,288   8,381   1,879

5. Circle the numbers with a 5 in the hundreds place.

   5,682   8,155   3,541   1,958   2,545   3,500

6. How do you mend a broken jack-o-lantern?

   _____
   _____

With a pumpkin patch.

Wake Up, Brain!!

Name: _____

Grammar

1. dear aunt kathy please bring uncle doug and come to my birthday party on may 26 at 4 oclock sincerely jenny

   _____
   _____
   _____
   _____

Spelling

Which is the correct word?

2. My bike is ___?___ . ☐ knew ☐ new ☐ gnu

3. This is ___?___ house. ☐ hour ☐ ower ☐ our

4. Turn ___?___ at the sign. ☐ right ☐ write ☐ rite

Language

Circle the words that have the sound of the letter.

5. | ŭ | run   ruin   bug   fun

6. | ā | bag   cake   pain   lamb

7. | ī | rise   grin   while   mine

Wake Up, Brain!!

Name: _____

Geography

Name one state that each river flows through or borders.

1. Columbia River _____

2. Ohio River _____

3. Yellowstone River _____

Math

Name the shapes.

4. ○ _____

5. ⬡ _____

6. △ _____

7. What kind of house is easiest to pick up?

_____

_____

A light house.

Wake Up, Brain!!

Name: _____

Grammar

1. my brother and me seen to dogs fighting it scareded me

   _____

   _____

2. jeremy didnt ran in the race tuesday he was sick with the flu

   _____

   _____

Spelling

Change these words to **ING** words.

3. ride _____

4. stop _____

5. wear _____

Language

6. In each blank, write the number 1, 2, 3, or 4 to put the sentences in the correct order.

   _____ Finally they finished!

   _____ Jenny and Joey planned to build a clubhouse.

   _____ They worked four days to build the clubhouse.

   _____ First they gathered wood and nails from Dad's shed.

Wake Up, Brain!!

Name: _____

Geography

1. If you had a meeting in the capital city of Bismark, in what state would you be?

    ❏ Nebraska ❏ North Dakota ❏ South Dakota

2. If you then traveled to the capital city of Minnesota, in what city would you be?

    ❏ Des Moines ❏ Minneapolis ❏ Madison

Math

3. You have $75.25 in your pocket before you go into the store. What do you have left after you buy these items? _____

    $ 15.00 $ 14.50 $ 32.25

4. What do wolves say when they are introduced to someone?

    _____
    _____

Howl do you do?

Wake Up, Brain!!

Name: _____

Grammar

1. ms kay jones   2752 sandy beach lane   georgetown south carolina 26555

   _____
   _____
   _____
   _____

Spelling

Change these words to **ING** words.

2. run _____
3. joke _____
4. swim _____

Language

Rewrite these sentences adding the missing noun or verb.

5. (Noun) picked up all the litter at the park.

   _____

6. The kids at the park (verb).

   _____

Wake Up, Brain!!

Name: _____

Geography

1. Fill in the missing words to "America the Beautiful."

   O beautiful for spacious _____, For amber waves of grain,

   For _____ mountain majesties, Above the fruited plain.

   America! America! God shed his _____ on thee, And crowned

   thy good with brotherhood, From sea to shining _____!

Math

2. Which months have only 30 days?

   _____ _____ _____ _____

3. How many months in three years?

   ☐ 6   ☐ 12   ☐ 36

4. What happened when the dog swallowed the watch?

   _____

   _____

He got a lot of ticks.

Wake Up, Brain!!

Name: _____

Grammar

1. do you know where them guys went to

   _____

   _____

2. she said she seen the same movie as i did but i dont think she did

   _____

   _____

Spelling

Underline the words that need a capital letter.

3. The golden gate bridge in california is long.

4. The twins, ben and ken, are at yellowstone park.

5. Who wrote the book mark twain?

Language

6. Jean runs faster than John but not as fast as Bill.

   Who runs the fastest? _____

7. Terry is older than Bob but younger than Kathy.

   Who is the oldest? _____

Wake Up, Brain!!

Name: _____

Geography

1. Is South Carolina closer to the Pacific or to the Atlantic Ocean?
   _____

2. Which continent has the most land?

   ☐ Asia   ☐ Africa

Math

Round the numbers to the nearest hundred.

3. 658 _____   4. 542 _____

5. 789 _____   6. 823 _____

7. 322 _____   8. 123 _____

9. If you dropped a tomato on your toe, would it hurt?
   _____
   _____

Only if it were in a can.

Wake Up, Brain!!

Name: _____

Grammar

1. do you like the movie titanic it has amazing photography

   _____

   _____

2. i think we have a math assignment due wednesday or thursday

   _____

   _____

Spelling

Which words are spelled correctly?

3. ☐ bewtiful   ☐ beautiful   ☐ beuatiful

4. ☐ people   ☐ poeple   ☐ peeple

5. ☐ wether   ☐ whather   ☐ whether

Language

Circle the sentences that tell a complete idea.

6. Sharks have an outer row of teeth.
7. Not a bone in its body.
8. Sharks cannot float.
9. In motion constantly.

Wake Up, Brain!!

Name: _____

Geography

1. What state capital has the same name as a famous explorer?

    ☐ Springfield   ☐ Columbus   ☐ Baton Rouge

2. What state is this city in? _____

Math

Write these phrases in money form (such as $5.38).

3. 6 dollars, 2 quarters, 3 dimes, 13 pennies _____

4. 2 10-dollar bills, 6 quarters, 4 nickels. _____

5. How much money all together? _____

6. What did the snow say to the field?

    _____
    _____

Do you catch my drift?

Wake Up, Brain!!

Name: _____

Grammar

1. what did kim mean when he said im infatuated with you

   _____

   _____

2. moms going to hit the ceiling when she sees this mess

   _____

   _____

Spelling

3. Write these words in alphabetical order.

outside	
other	
offer	
open	

Language

Complete the sentence with the bolded word's opposite.

4. I got out of bed very _____. **early**

5. The feathers made my pillow _____. **hard**

6. The clown's _____ was painted on. **frown**

Wake Up, Brain!!

Name: _____

Geography

1. In what part of the U.S. is Minnesota located?

   ❐ east   ❐ west   ❐ north

2. How many states are north of the equator?

   ❐ 40   ❐ 45   ❐ 50

Math

3. Complete the parttern.

   13, 16, 19, _____ , _____ , _____ , _____ , _____ , _____ ,

4. Which group is counting by sixes?

   ❐   12, 16, 24, 30

   ❐   12, 18, 24, 30

5. Why did the belt go to jail?

   _____

   _____

It held up a pair of pants.

Wake Up, Brain!!

Name: _____

Grammar

1. she gots a new computer in her bedroom now shell do all her homework there
   _____
   _____

2. i dont know nothing about daffodils carnations or pansies I just no about soccer and baseball
   _____
   _____

Spelling

Choose the correct word in the parentheses.

3. I need to go (buy, by) Joe's gift. _____

4. Please (right, write) me a letter. _____

5. (There, Their) you are! _____

Language

Underline the sentences that do NOT show reality.

6. Soup was cooking on the stove.
7. The basket bent over and picked up the glass.
8. Annie drew a picture of a sunny beach.
9. The car took us to the mall without the engine running.

Wake Up, Brain!!

Name: _____

Geography

1. Which state probably has a desert?

    ☐ Alaska   ☐ Arizona   ☐ Alabama

2. What state is made up of several islands?

    ☐ Alaska   ☐ Florida   ☐ Hawaii

Math

Shade in the fraction.

3. 2/3   4. 1/3   5. 3/4

6. Why did the kitten want to be a nurse?

   _____
   _____

She wanted to be a first-aid kit.

Wake Up, Brain!!

Name: _____

Grammar

1. did you have fun on your trip to disneyland

   _____

   _____

2. the policeman aint never going to catch that dog

   _____

   _____

Spelling

Spell the antonym for each word.

3. up _____

4. wild _____

5. old _____

Language

Underline the simple subject of each sentence.

6. Ted liked to use markers.

7. Mom drove us here in her new car.

8. The phone call was for you.

Wake Up, Brain!!

Name: _____

Geography

1. In what state will you find the city of Santa Fe?

   ❏ New Jersey   ❏ New Mexico   ❏ New York

2. You're going on vacation to your aunt's house in Baton Rouge. What state are you going to?

   ❏ Louisiana   ❏ Georgia   ❏ Utah

Math

3. There are 75 pencils in the box. Mr. Wagner bought 122 more. Show your work to find the answer.

4. Thirty-six ducks are sitting in a pond. Ninety-four more land in the pond but 12 leave. Show your work to find the answer.

5. What did one math book say to the other?

   _____

   _____

I have a lot of problems.

Wake Up, Brain!!

Name: _____

Grammar

1. steve werent able to come to dans birthday party last saturday

   _____

   _____

2. does you like to go to bennys buger barn for his famous big benny burger

   _____

   _____

Spelling

Which words are spelled correctly?

3. ☐ whole   ☐ hole   ☐ hoole

4. ☐ thier   ☐ there   ☐ their

5. ☐ where   ☐ whear   ☐ wear

Language

Fill in rhyming words to finish these poems.

6. She fell into the bathtub,
   She fell into the sink.
   She fell into the raspberry jam
   And came out _____.

7. I never saw a purple cow,
   I never hope to see one.
   But I can tell you anyhow,
   I'd rather see than be _____.

Wake Up, Brain!!

Name: _____

Geography

1. What major river flows into the Mississippi River just north of St. Louis?

    ☐ Illinois River   ☐ Missouri River

2. What is the capital of Florida?

    ☐ Tallahassee   ☐ Orlando   ☐ Miami

Math

3. [array of smiley faces] + [array of smiley faces] = _____

4. What is the clumsiest bee?

   _____

   _____

A bumbling bee.

Wake Up, Brain!!

Name: _____

Grammar

1. brian jones taked a plane to california on tuesday hell be back friday

   _____
   _____

2. can we read the poem march wind aloud or should we read silently

   _____
   _____

Spelling

Which spelling of these double-vowel words is correct?

3. ❒ deosn't ❒ doesn't
4. ❒ through ❒ thruogh
5. ❒ waether ❒ weather

Language

Circle the words that have the sound of the letter in the box.

6. $\bar{e}$ — week   wet   street   let's   succeed
7. $\breve{o}$ — dog   off   do   chop   zoo
8. $\bar{u}$ — rug   clue   truck   mule   hurt

Wake Up, Brain!!

Name: _____

Geography

1. What are the four geographic directions on a compass?

   _____   _____

   _____   _____

2. Large bodies of land on Earth are called _____.

Math

Draw the clock hands to show the time plus 20 minutes.

3. 11:26   4. 7:48   5. 1:19

6. Why did the little boy examine all his animal crackers before he ate them?

   _____

   _____

He was checking to see if the seal was broken.

Wake Up, Brain!!

Name: _____

Grammar

1. i gived mrs bailey my math homework she was proud of me

   _____

   _____

2. georges dad gave him a subscription to sports illustrated for kids for his birthday

   _____

   _____

Spelling

3. Write these words in alphabetical order. | not   our   are   too   out   to |

Language

Circle the word with the same or almost the same meaning as the bolded word.

4. birthday **present**   now   pain   gift

5. **bright** idea   dumb   smart   confusing

6. **scurry** away   run   look   eat

Wake Up, Brain!!

Name: _____

Geography

Identify these states by their unusual shapes.

1. _____   2. _____

Math

What time will it be in 45 minutes?

3. _____   4. _____

5. What do you call a crab who plays baseball?
   _____
   _____

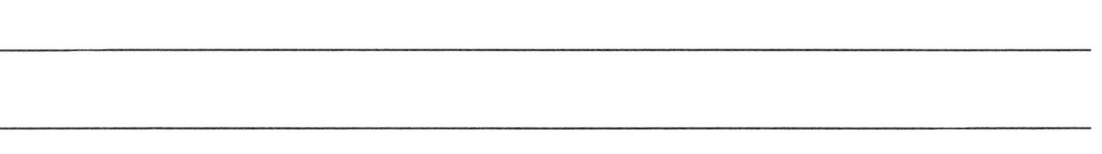

A pinch hitter.

Wake Up, Brain!!

Name: _____

Grammar

1. he gots a new book about dinosaurs

   _____

   _____

2. carls dad was like i dont have no gum

   _____

   _____

Spelling

Make a new word by changing the first one or two letters of the bolded word.

3. **know** _____

4. **black** _____

5. **round** _____

Language

Unscramble the words to find things you can ride.

6. nairt _____

7. keib _____

8. taob _____

Wake Up, Brain!!

Name: _____

Geography

1. What is the capital city of Arizona?
   _____

2. If your friend moves to the east coast capital city of Albany, to what state has he or she moved?
   _____

Math

3. You have $25.00. How much is left after you buy these items?
   _____

   $3.09 $1.85 $15.35

4. Why did the girl spray bug killer on her clock?
   _____
   _____

It was full of ticks.

Wake Up, Brain!!

Name: _____

Grammar

1. youve gots to walk your dog sugar every day said mom

   _____

   _____

2. may i please have a swimming party for the 4th of july i will only invite 40 kids

   _____

   _____

Spelling

Which word should be used in the sentence?

3. The _____ cleaned our room.   ❏ made   ❏ maid

4. I don't know _____ to go.   ❏ whether   ❏ weather

5. Jay ate the _____ thing.   ❏ hole   ❏ whole

Language

Which word fits in both sentences?

6. Every student must have a _____ to go to the library.
   That red car will _____ us in just a minute.
      ❏ friend   ❏ pass   ❏ note

7. In October the _____ fall from the trees. The bus _____ the school at 2:45.
      ❏ kids   ❏ apples   ❏ leaves

Wake Up, Brain!!

Name: _____

Geography

1. ☐ True ☐ False A sea is usually larger than an ocean.

2. ☐ True ☐ False Land completely surrounded by water is an island.

3. ☐ True ☐ False If you are facing west, north is to your left.

Math

4. How many cups in 2 pints? _____

5. How many pints in 3 quarts? _____

6. How many quarts in 5 gallons? _____

7. What do you call a computer injury?
_____
_____

A mega bite.

Wake Up, Brain!!

Name: _____

Grammar

1. mother said i have to practice my piano lesson for ½ hours every single morning

   _____

   _____

2. will you please help me with my math and history

   _____

   _____

Spelling

Add ING to these words.

3. play _____

4. come _____

5. snap _____

Language

Which best describes the suffix bolded in the word?

6. hazard**ous**   ☐ without   ☐ every   ☐ full of

7. month**ly**   ☐ without   ☐ every   ☐ full of

8. help**less**   ☐ without   ☐ every   ☐ full of

84   Wake Up, Brain!! • Grade 4   ECS Learning Systems, Inc.   All rights reserved

Wake Up, Brain!!

Name: _____

Geography

1. What country is Mexico's closest northern neighbor?

    ☐ France ☐ U.S. ☐ Canada

2. Which two oceans border Europe?

    ☐ Arctic, Indian ☐ Atlantic, Indian ☐ Atlantic, Arctic

Math

3. Compute.

    $$\begin{array}{ccc} 7 & 6 & 5 \\ \times 5 & \times 5 & \times 5 \\ \hline \end{array}$$

4. Why is Alabama the smartest state?

    _____

    _____

It has four A's and one B.

Wake Up, Brain!!

Name: _____

Grammar

1. jenny went too bed early so her could help deliver papers with dj

   _____
   _____

2. was that phone call for me who was it

   _____
   _____

Spelling

Rewrite these words and underline all the vowels.

3. beautiful _____
4. through _____
5. because _____

Language

What is the root word?

6. teacher _____
7. watchful _____
8. sinkable _____

86 Wake Up, Brain!! • Grade 4   ECS Learning Systems, Inc.   All rights reserved

Wake Up, Brain!!

Name: _____

Geography

1. ☐ True   ☐ False   The Rio Grande River forms the boundary between Mexico and Texas.

2. ☐ True   ☐ False   The Atlantic Ocean is the largest ocean in the world.

Math

3. What is the difference between 287 and 329?
   _____

4. What is the difference between 891 and 233?
   _____

5. What is a bud that doesn't bloom?
   _____
   _____

Your tastebuds.

Wake Up, Brain!!

Name: _____

Grammar

1. what is your favorite season i like summer the best

   _____

   _____

2. christmas is my favorite holiday whats yours

   _____

   _____

Spelling

Which word is spelled correctly?

3. ☐ wouldnt ☐ woodn't ☐ wouldn't

4. ☐ doesn't ☐ dozent ☐ doesnt

5. ☐ terribel ☐ terrible ☐ terible

Language

6. Draw a line between the rhyming words.

wind	wrong
tree	mole
hole	float
great	kind
boat	knee
song	plate

Wake Up, Brain!!

Name: _____

Geography

1. Which ocean is north of Alaska?

    ❏ Arctic   ❏ Asian   ❏ Atlantic

2. Which river is longer?

    ❏ Colorado   ❏ Mississippi

Math

What time will it be in 35 minutes?

3. _____   4. _____

5. What goes in one ear and out the other?
   _____
   _____

A worm in a cornfield.

Wake Up, Brain!!

Name: _____

Grammar

1. is your appointment with dr nelson at 230 today or tomorrow

   _____
   _____

2. he gots more juice than i did is that fair

   _____
   _____

Spelling

3. Circle the letters that make the sound of **K**.

       cake   know   car   Christmas

4. Circle the letters that make the sound of **J**.

       giant   junk   age   edge

Language

5. Underline any noun in this sentence.

   It was so hot today that we went to the beach.

6. Underline any verb in this sentence.

   Mom needs to go to the grocery store today.

Wake Up, Brain!!

Name: _____

Geography

1. What is the state capital of Delaware?
   _____

2. What is the capital of Mexico?
   _____

Math

3. Compute.

      3   3   3   3
   X 4   X 8   X 9   X 6

4. Write a four digit number with 9 in the tens place.
   _____

5. What kind of ears do engines have?
   _____
   _____

Engineers.

Wake Up, Brain!!

Name: _____

Grammar

1. she seen the lincoln school directory on the desk and slipped it into her backpack

   _____
   _____

2. we was going to lunch together but dad surprised me and took me

   _____
   _____

Spelling

Which word is spelled correctly?

3. ☐ scate ☐ scait ☐ skate

4. ☐ brothar ☐ brother ☐ bruther

5. ☐ writing ☐ writting ☐ writeing

Language

6. Underline the words that come between **germ** and **girl** in the dictionary.

   get give ghost giant

   grin gal genius giraffe

Wake Up, Brain!!

Name: _____

Geography

1. Shade in North America.

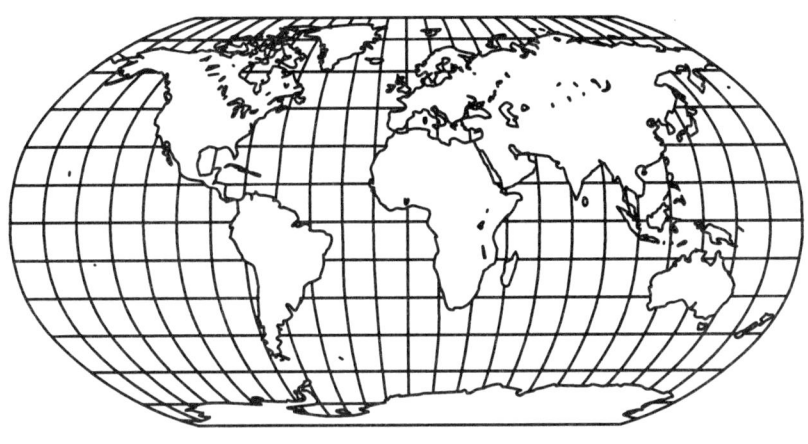

Math

Draw hands to show the correct time.

2. 7:57   3. 2:23

4. Why did the man put cheese on his computer?

_____
_____

He wanted to feed the mouse.

Wake Up, Brain!!

Name: _____

Grammar

1. my parents are proud of my report card i improved a lot
   _____
   _____

2. it was sharons bike he was riding when he had his wreck
   _____
   _____

Spelling

Which word goes in the sentence?

3. I have to _____ a letter to grandma.   ❏ write   ❏ right

4. My old dog can't _____ very well any more.   ❏ here   ❏ hear

Language

What kind of sentences are these?

5. She can mow the lawn.
   ❏ command   ❏ statement   ❏ question

6. Can she mow the lawn?
   ❏ command   ❏ statement   ❏ question

7. Mow the lawn.
   ❏ command   ❏ statement   ❏ question

94   Wake Up, Brain!! • Grade 4   ECS Learning Systems, Inc.   All rights reserved

Wake Up, Brain!!

Name: _____

Geography

1. Color your home state red. If you were born in a different state, color it blue.

Math

Write the numbers.

2. Eight hundred sixty three _____

3. Twenty one dollars and fourteen cents _____

4. One thousand twenty two _____

5. Why did the bear run around the bed?
   _____
   _____

He wanted to catch up on his sleep.

Wake Up, Brain!!

Name: _____

Grammar

1. tom and me are going to the ball game with jim do you wanna come along

   _____

   _____

2. donna asked if she could use jennys dress for the party

   _____

   _____

Spelling

3. Circle the letters that make the f sound.

elephant	enough	through	laugh
telephone	ghost	cough	giraffe

4. Check in at home every _____.   ❑ our   ❑ hour

Language

   CROOK – 1. a hook; 2. a bend or curve; 3. a thief.

5. How many meanings are there for crook? _____

6. The road had a *crook* in it. Which meaning describes how crook is used in this sentence? _____

7. Write another word for the 3rd meaning. _____

Wake Up, Brain!!

Name: _____

Geography

Name these states from the Northwest.

1. _____
2. _____
3. _____

Math

Measure these lines in inches and write the number in the blank space.

4. _____ inches

5. _____ inches

6. _____ inches

7. What do you get when you cross a pig with a Christmas tree?
_____
_____

A porcupine.

Wake Up, Brain!!

Name: _____

Grammar

1. we didn't catched him he ran to faster

   _____

   _____

2. can grace buy my old rollerblades for 5 dollars and 30 cents

   _____

   _____

Spelling

3. Underline the three misspleled words below. Spell them correctly in the boxes.

   I made my mom a beautifull card for her birthday. She was writting me a thank you note when I walked into the room. She gave me a bigg hug instead.

Language

Write a short sentence for each kind of sentence.

4. COMMAND _____

5. QUESTION _____

6. STATEMENT _____

Wake Up, Brain!!

Name: _____

Geography

1. Color Texas.

Math

2. If you had $125.00, check all the items you could buy without spending all your money.

☐ $45.00   ☐ $38.00   ☐ $28.00   ☐ $19.00

3. Which is the left side of the pie?
   _____
   _____

The side that is not eaten.

Wake Up, Brain!!

Name: _____

Grammar

1. she drunk the pepsi two fast

   _____

   _____

2. my family is moving to des moines iowa after christmas

   _____

   _____

Spelling

Which word is spelled correctly?

3. ☐ prety   ☐ pretty   ☐ preety

4. ☐ those   ☐ thuse   ☐ thoose

5. ☐ zu   ☐ zue   ☐ zoo

Language

Finish these analogies.

6. **sight** is to **eye** as **sound** is to _____

7. **word** is to **sentence** as **page** is to _____

8. **top** is to **bottom** as **over** is to _____

100   Wake Up, Brain!! • Grade 4   ECS Learning Systems, Inc.   All rights reserved

Wake Up, Brain!!

Name: _____

Geography

1. What state is shaded?

   _____

Math

2. Color the fifth shape red, circle the second shape, and color the seventh shape yellow.

3. Compute.

      3   4   5   3
   X 4   X 7   X 6   X 8

4. Why didn't the bulb turn on when the switch was flipped?

   _____
   _____

It was a tulip bulb.

Wake Up, Brain!!

Name: _____

Grammar

1. can i eat with joel they are having pizza from tonys and its my favorite

   _____
   _____

2. i asked rebecca to call me but she didnt i wonder what happened

   _____
   _____

Spelling

3. Put these words in alphabetical order.

   | gym | people | did | kick | and | your |

   _____   _____
   _____   _____
   _____   _____

Language

Which is the correct verb?

4. Patrick   ❏ ran   ❏ run   all the way from home.

5. Chris' birthday ❏ is   ❏ was   tomorrow.

6. Michael   ❏ buyed   ❏ bought   her a nice gift.

Wake Up, Brain!!

Name: _____

Geography

1. What state is shaded?

   _____

Math

2. Draw lines to divide these shapes into fourths.

3. What is the sum of 28 and 55? _____

4. Why don't turkeys eat very much?

   _____
   _____

Because they are always stuffed.

Wake Up, Brain!!

Name: _____

Grammar

1. the boys in the neighborhood built a clubhouse this summer

   _____

   _____

2. have you ever gone to camp miniteepee its so much fun

   _____

   _____

Spelling

3. Put these words in alphabetical order.

   | thing   talk   truck   then   two   tell |

   _____   _____
   _____   _____
   _____   _____

Language

Write the sequences from **least** to **greatest**.

4. nickel, quarter, dime _____

5. teenager, man, baby _____

6. hour, second, minute _____

Wake Up, Brain!!

Name: _____

Geography

1. What state is shaded?

    _____

Math

What time will it be in two and a half hours?

2. _____   3. _____

4. What did the hippie pencil say to the hippie paper?

   _____
   _____

Write on, man!

Answer Key

Note: Grammar activities may occasionally have more than one possible answer.

Page 6
1. Jamie ate all the Ben and Jerry's ice cream.
2. Do you have time to take a shower before we go?
3. gym
4. favorite
5. thought
6. out
7. bottom
8. month

Page 7
1. east
2. United States
3. No
4. Yes; $2.00 change

Page 8
1. Let's have soup, sandwiches, and chips for Saturday's lunch.
2. I can't seem to keep my room clean. Can you?
3. house, home
4. car, automobile
5. teacher, principal
6. Answers will vary but should be maintained within the stated categories.

Page 9
1. Indianapolis
2. Nevada, Arizona
3. $18.00
4. $12.00

Page 10
1. She and her family invited me to go to church with them.
2. We saw the President of the United States at the parade.
3. girl
4. truck
5. mail
6. Iguanodons lived on Earth.
7. plants
8. like leather

Page 11
1. A star
2. 7
3. $1.85
4. $179.00 (179 dollars)

Page 12
1. We'll go the California this summer. We might go to Disneyland, too.
2. My chores are to take out the trash, make my bed, mow the lawn, and walk the dog.
3. everything; doesn't; except
4. Kareem Abdul-Jabbar played basketball.
5. in high school and college

Page 13
1. blue
2. water
3. triangle and circle

Page 14
1. Why don't we go see <u>Dr. Doolittle</u> together? We'd have a great time.
2. Please put those pencils in the box, those books on the shelves, and the papers in the trash.
3. right
4. found
5. Answers will vary but should be maintained within the stated categories.

Page 15
1. warmer
2. border
3. $7.00
4. $8.00

Page 16
1. Julie and I were going to the mall to shop for school clothes.
2. We drank too much pop and got a bellyache.
3. trouble
4. doesn't
5. excited
6. biting, feeling, says, lied

Page 17
1. land
2. the equator
3. 90 (94 − 5 + 1)
4. 2 pints
5. 4 gallons

Page 18
1. My uncle has an orchard with peach trees, apple trees, and lemon trees.
2. Have you seen the movie called <u>A Bug's Life</u>?
3. flower, fun, frame, flown
4. make, slice, stir, sprinkle

Page 19
1. Antarctica, North America, South America, Asia, Europe, Africa, Australia
2. 2:15 (first clock)

Page 20
1. We ran around the whole playground four times.
2. Keith and Erin don't like pickles. Jim only likes them on hamburgers. I love them on everything.
3. golden
4. racket
5. box
6. story
7. soft

Page 21
1. No
2. California
3. Shapes are: sphere, cone, circle, cylinder, square, triangle, cube.

Page 22
1. Did you know he hid the car behind the tree? I can't believe we didn't find it!
2. She drank all her milk at dinner and then asked for more later.
3. outside
4. especially
5. sometime
6. forest – woods
7. sleepy – tired
8. jacket – coat
9. ran – jogged

Page 23
1. Pacific, Atlantic, Arctic, Indian
2. 48
3. 44
4. 269

Answer Key

5. 110
6. 124

Page 24
1. My cats love to wrestle and hiss at each other. It looks like fighting, but it's not.
2. Are your grandparents arriving on the 6:00 a.m. flight?
3. graph
4. elephant
5. phone or telephone
6. unusual – mammal
7. webbed – feet

Page 25
1. an island
2. Atlantic, Arctic
3. 196
4. 3048

Page 26
1. At summer camp, we all rode horses except Frank. He'd been bucked off before and was afraid.
2. "Those cars are going to crash!" yelled James. "Watch out!"
3. can't
4. doesn't
5. wouldn't
6. School
7. Vegetables
8. Dogs (or Breeds)

Page 27
1. Antarctica
2. ocean
3. clock should show 4:17
4. clock should show 12:09

Page 28
1. Grace and I went to see Joel's new bike. It's a cool racing bike.
2. "Teresa brought her lunch today," said Kim. "Did you?"
3. about
4. before
5. myself
6. Two sentences should be properly written and punctuated and contain the words "sports" and "other."

Page 29
1. Bering
2. Mexico
3. today
4. circle, square, 5-point star, 4-point star, triangle.

Page 30
1. He drank all the milk and ate all the cookies. He must have been very hungry.
2. He drew that picture all by himself without ever looking up.
3. didn't
4. let's
5. they're
6. twenty, forty, sixty
7. least, same, most
8. quarter, half, whole

Page 31
1. west
2. Atlantic, Pacific, Arctic
3. 45
4. 230

Page 32
1. David has a ferret, and Michael has a guinea pig.
2. Rebecca has gone to Oregon for the summer. She'll be back in September.
3. write
4. teacher
5. children (children, teacher, write)
6. yard
7. September
8. sixth

Page 33
1. Pacific
2. Asia, Europe
3. hexagon
4. octagon
5. trapezoid

Page 34
1. She did her chores every day and knew her mom would be happy.
2. "Where did you go this weekend?" asked Ben. "We went camping," replied Eddie.
3. your, you're
4. there, their
5. plan
6. Answers will vary but both sentences must contain a verb/noun combination word.

Page 35
1. Kansas
2. Oregon
3. Lexington
4. (–)
5. (+)
6. (–)
7. (+)

Page 36
1. Linda doesn't have a pencil box. Is it okay if she uses a pouch?
2. He did his homework very well/real well.
3. running
4. coming
5. adding
6. The dog got out when the boy opened the gate.
7. I divided my apple in half because I saw Tim wanted some.

Page 37
1. Alaska
2. New York
3. 3 (466, 555, 501)
4. 10

Page 38
1. Patrick has to practice his piano lessons every night for thirty minutes.
2. Donald went all by himself to the mall, and he got lost.
3. shared
4. chopped
5. spied
6. We're
7. can't
8. Don't

Page 39
1. Nevada
2. North Dakota

Answer Key

3. 3 (3,010; 2,190; 4,390)
4. 42

Page 40
1. Can we go to Tony's house in Tallahassee on the Fourth of July?
2. Mary has two assignments ready to turn in.
3. know
4. buy
5. threw
6. Flowers
7. Fruits
8. Times

Page 41
1. Springfield
2. Yes, Alaska
3. (scale)
4. (ruler)

Page 42
1. Can you bring your book, a CD, and some pop to the party?
2. My cat, Tigger, is like a wild cat when he eats catnip.
3. sure
4. friend
5. would
6. his
7. think
8. want

Page 43
1. Proper location of the directional abbreviations
2. A red mark must appear at the 5½ mark on the ruler.
3. A blue mark must appear at the 2¾ mark on the ruler.

Page 44
1. She doesn't want any because she's finished.
2. "Did you get home late last night?" asked Mom. Ben said, "Just by 15 minutes, Mom."
3. rain
4. good
5/7. Answers will vary but must indicate an adjective for each sentence.

Page 45
1. Florida
2. California
3. 372
4. 250
5. 8

Page 46
1. I used all my paper. Can I have more?
2. I'll pay you 25 cents a paper, but I only have $5.00.
3. sometime
4. thought
5. weather
6. not
7. without
8. opposite of

Page 47
1. Wyoming
2. Maine
3. triangle, octagon

Page 48
1. We wrote a note asking Brandon who he liked the most.
2. Karen had her feelings hurt because John said, "Go away!"
3. eat
4. small
5. birds
6. He
7. Rabbits

Page 49
1. west
2. Nashville
3. 3 angles, 3 sides
4. 4 angles, 4 sides
5. 8 angles, 8 sides

Page 50
1. We saw the new baby panda at the zoo in June.
2. We've had fun, but now we have to go.
3. sister
4. outside
5. especially
6. pulled
7. stopped
8. gave

Page 51
1. California
2. Tennessee, North Carolina
3. hexagon, circle

Page 52
1. It is too early to wake up, so I'll stay in bed another hour.
2. Did you laugh at Bill's joke? I didn't think it was funny.
3/5. Answers will vary but must reflect a word opposite of those listed.
6. Answers will vary, but sentences should be correctly written, represent the children rollerblading, and have nouns correctly underlined.

Page 53
1. Russia
2. east
3. 10 cm
4. 7 cm
5. 8 cm

Page 54
1. Would you rather use the computer or a calculator?
2. Where has Toby hidden his bone? He keeps digging more holes.
3. night
4. write
5. right
6. a c t a r c j w c s
   k h m b p m l s d t
   w i r n o i s e t a
   c n i r s p i d e r

Page 55
1. Nebraska
2. 94
3. 93

Page 56
1. Don't you wish those kittens belonged to you and me?
2. Stephanie said, "We're going to go to the mall."
3. wanted
4. told
5. excited
6. bag, match

Answer Key

7. bread, wet, red
8. phone, grow

Page 57
1. Snake River
2. Mississippi River
3. Yukon River
4. 8,989; 5,181; 3,288; 8,381
5. 3,541; 2,545; 3,500

Page 58
1. Dear Aunt Kathy,
   Please bring Uncle Doug and come to my birthday party on May 26 at 4 o'clock.
   Sincerely, Jenny
2. new
3. our
4. right
5. run, bug, fun
6. cake, pain
7. rise, while, mine

Page 59
1. OR, WA
2. OH, WV, PA, KY, IN, or IL
3. WY, MT, or ND
4. circle
5. cube
6. pyramid

Page 60
1. My brother and I saw two dogs fighting. It scared me.
2. Jeremy didn't run in the race Tuesday. He was sick with the flu.
3. riding
4. stopping
5. wearing
6. 4, 1, 3, 2

Page 61
1. North Dakota
2. Minneapolis
3. $13.50

Page 62
1. Ms. Kay Jones
   2752 Sandy Beach Lane
   Georgetown, SC 26555
2. running
3. joking
4. swimming
5. Answers will vary but must be a fitting noun for the sentence.
6. Answers will vary but must be a fitting verb for the sentence.

Page 63
1. skies, purple, grace, sea
2. September, April, June, November
3. 36

Page 64
1. Do you know where those guys went?
2. She said she saw the same movie I did, but I don't think she did.
3. Golden Gate Bridge, California
4. Ben, Ken, Yellowstone Park
5. Mark Twain
6. Bill
7. Kathy

Page 65
1. Atlantic
2. Asia
3. 700
4. 500
5. 800
6. 800
7. 300
8. 100

Page 66
1. Did you like the movie <u>Titanic</u>? It had amazing photography!
2. I think we have a math assignment due Wednesday or Thursday.
3. beautiful
4. people
5. whether
6. (Complete idea.)
7. (Incomplete idea.)
8. (Complete idea.)
9. (Incomplete idea.)

Page 67
1. Columbus
2. Ohio
3. $6.93
4. $21.70
5. $28.63

Page 68
1. What did Kim mean when he said, "I'm infatuated with you."
2. Mom's going to hit the ceiling when she sees this mess!
3. offer, open, other, outside
4. late
5. soft
6. smile, grin

Page 69
1. North
2. 50
3. 22, 25, 28, 31, 34, 37
4. 12, 18, 24, 30

Page 70
1. She has a new computer in her bedroom. Now she'll do all her homework there.
2. I don't know anything about daffodils, carnations, or pansies. I just know about soccer and baseball.
3. buy
4. write
5. There
6. (Not underlined)
7. (Underlined)
8. (Not underlined)
9. (Underlined)

Page 71
1. Arizona
2. Hawaii
3. 2 of 3 blocks should be shaded.
4. 1 of 3 blocks should be shaded.
5. 3 of 4 blocks should be shaded.

Page 72
1. Did you have fun on your trip to Disneyland?
2. The policeman isn't ever going to catch that dog.
3. down
4. tame
5. new
6. Ted
7. Mom
8. call

Answer Key

Page 73
1. New Mexico
2. Louisiana
3. 197
4. 118

Page 74
1. Steve wasn't able to come to Dan's birthday party last Saturday.
2. Do you like to go to Benny's Burger Barn for his famous Big Benny Burger?
3. whole, hole
4. there, their
5. where, wear
6. pink
7. one

Page 75
1. Missouri River
2. Tallahassee
3. 100

Page 76
1. Brian Jones took a plane to California on Tuesday. He'll be back Friday.
2. Can we read the poem <u>March Wind</u> aloud or should we read silently?
3. doesn't
4. through
5. weather
6. week, street, succeed
7. dog, chop, off
8. clue, mule

Page 77
1. north, south, east, west
2. continents
   Clock hands should show:
3/5. 11:46, 8:08, 1:39

Page 78
1. I gave Mrs. Bailey my math homework. She was proud of me.
2. George's dad gave him a subscription to <u>Sports Illustrated for Kids</u> for his birthday.
3. are, not, our, out, to, too
4. gift
5. smart

6. run

Page 79
1. Texas
2. Nevada
3. 12:10
4. 1:00

Page 80
1. He has a new book about dinosaurs.
2. Carl's dad said, "I don't have any gum."
3. Answers will vary (e.g., snow, grow).
4. Answers will vary (e.g., crack, clack).
5. Answers will vary (e.g., found, sound).
6. train
7. bike
8. boat

Page 81
1. Phoenix
2. New York
3. $4.71

Page 82
1. "You've got to walk your dog, Sugar, every day," said Mom.
2. May I please have a swimming party for the 4th of July? I will only invite 40 kids.
3. maid
4. whether
5. whole
6. pass
7. leaves

Page 83
1. F
2. T
3. F
4. 4
5. 6
6. 20

Page 84
1. Mother said I have to practice my piano lesson for half an hour

every single morning.
2. Will you please help me with my math and history?
3. playing
4. coming
5. snapping
6. full of
7. every
8. without

Page 85
1. U.S.
2. Atlantic, Arctic
3. 35
4. 30
5. 25

Page 86
1. Jenny went to bed early so she could help deliver papers with D.J.
2. Was that phone call for me? Who was it?
3. b e <u>a</u> u t i f u l
4. t h r <u>o</u> u g h
5. b e c <u>a</u> u s e
6. teach
7. watch
8. sink

Page 87
1. T
2. F
3. 42
4. 658

Page 88
1. What is your favorite season? I like summer the best.
2. Christmas is my favorite holiday. What's yours?
3. wouldn't
4. doesn't
5. terrible
6. wind–kind
   tree–knee
   hole–mole
   great–plate
   boat–float
   song–wrong

Page 89
1. Arctic
2. Mississippi

Answer Key

3. 8:35
4. 5:05

Page 90
1. Is your appointment with Dr. Nelson at 2:30 today or tomorrow?
2. He got more juice than I did. Is that fair?
3. ca(k)e, (c)ar, (Ch)ristmas
4. (g)iant, (j)unk, (a)ge, e(dg)e
5. beach
6. needs, go

Page 91
1. Dover
2. Mexico City
3. 12, 24, 27, 18
4. Answers will vary but must have a 9 in the 10's place

Page 92
1. She saw the Lincoln School Directory on the desk and slipped it into her backpack.
2. We were going to lunch together, but Dad surprised me and took me.
3. skate
4. brother
5. writing
6. get, ghost, giant, giraffe

Page 93
1. North America should be properly shaded.
2. Clock hands should be drawn to reflect 7:57.
3. Clock hands should be drawn to reflect 2:23.

Page 94
1. My parents are proud of my report card. I improved a lot.
2. He was riding Sharon's bike when he had his wreck.
3. write
4. hear
5. statement
6. question
7. command

Page 95
1. The student's home state and state of birth should be shaded.
2. 863
3. $21.14
4. 1,022

Page 96
1. Tom and I are going to the ball game with Jim. Do you want to come along?
2. Donna asked if she could use Jenny's dress for the party.
3. ele(ph)ant, enou(gh)t, lau(gh), tele(ph)one, cou(gh), gira(ff)e
4. hour
5. 3
6. 2
7. Answers should contain proper usage of "crook" as it refers to a thief.

Page 97
1. Washington
2. Idaho
3. Oregon
4. 2 inches
5. 3¾ inches
6. 2½ inches

Page 98
1. We didn't catch him. He ran too fast.
2. Can Grace buy my old rollerblades for $5.30?
3. beautiful, writing, big
4. Answers will vary but must be in the structure of a command.
5. Answers will vary but must be in the structure of a question.
6. Answers will vary but must be in the structure of a statement.

Page 99
1. The state of Texas must be colored in.
2. Any three items may be checked.

Page 100
1. She drank the Pepsi too fast.
2. My family is moving to Des Moines, Iowa, after Christmas.
3. pretty
4. those
5. zoo
6. ear
7. book
8. under

Page 101
1. Utah
2. diamond - circled; house shape - colored red; star - colored yellow, 4th
3. 12, 28, 30, 24

Page 102
1. Can I eat with Joel? They are having pizza from Tony's and it's my favorite.
2. I asked Rebecca to call me, but she didn't. I wonder what happened.
3. and, did, gym, kick, people, your
4. ran
5. is
6. bought

Page 103
1. West Virginia
2. Each shape should be divided in equal fourths with horizontal and vertical lines.
3. 83

Page 104
1. The boys in the neighborhood built a clubhouse this summer.
2. Have you ever gone to Camp Miniteepee? It's so much fun.
3. talk, tell, then, think, truck, two
4. nickel, dime, quarter
5. baby, teenager, man
6. second, minute, hour

Page 105
1. Tennessee
2. 10:00
3. 2:30

About the Authors

After graduating from the University of Utah, **Michelle Ball** (right) lived in Salt Lake City before returning to her hometown of Idaho Falls, Idaho. She has three children, Conrad, Rebecca, and Patrick. Her husband, Doug, is a great support in her life and has always valued her love for teaching. He is an active part of her school life and known in the neighborhood as "Mrs. Ball's Husband."

Michelle's 15 years of teaching experiences in kindergarten, second, and third grades provided a sound foundation for her current position as a teacher in a multi-age classroom. "Teaching three grades at once has definitely enhanced my life (my dear friend and co-author's daughter was my student). Working in a multi-age classroom has provided opportunities to develop organizational skills and teaching strategies that benefit my students. Working with children has given me countless joys. My students have enriched my life beyond measure."

Barbara Morris (left) grew up and received her education in Idaho. A career in banking took her to Utah and California before she and her husband, Tony, became parents and moved back "home" to Idaho to raise their only child, Jennifer. As a new parent, "Barb" developed her own publishing skills and eventually built a small, in-home desktop publishing business.

Barb met Michelle as she enrolled Jennifer in Michelle's multi-grade classroom. Eventually, their relationship developed into a bond of friendship that enhanced both lives and fulfilled their individual goals and dreams. As a full-time office manager for a local hospital, Barb had little time to volunteer in the classroom, but had a desire to stay involved with her child's education. She offered her desktop publishing skills to Michelle, who sketched out student worksheets, literature studies, and classroom management tools. Barb converted them into the original student-friendly and teacher-helpful *Wake Up, Brain!!*, which developed into the new series for grades 1 through 6.